The Regius Poem or Halliwell Manuscript

Translated by James O. Halliwell

Edited by Carl E. Weaver

Cover: King Athelstan (Aethelstan). Unknown artist, line engraving, late 18th to early 19th century. Owned by the National Portrait Gallery in London

ISBN: 978-1-944616-00-7
Copyright © 2016 by Broken Column Press. All Rights reserved.
BrokenColumnPress.com

Introduction

The Regius Poem, also known as the Halliwell Manuscript, is a long series of rhyming couplets that make up what is thought to be the earliest of the Old Charges of Masonry. It was discovered in the British Museum by James O. Halliwell in 1838. While sometimes thought to have been written during the reign of King Athelstan (924-940 A.D.), the document actually dates to the late 14th century. Whether it is a derivative work based on a separate manuscript from Athelstan's time is unknown.

However, the Regius Poem is the cornerstone of the Legend of York, detailing how King Athelstan organized the operative masons in England and ordered that an annual assembly of masons be held in York. The king also established the first grand lodge of masons, and put his brother, Prince Edwin, at the head of it. These were likely all operative workmen. However, what is interesting is that, as scholars and patrons of the craft, Athelstan and Edwin were likely among the first speculative masons in England.

This manuscript also outlines how Masons should act toward each other and toward the civil magistrate. It also talks about the history and philosophy of the order of Masons.

The poem is a 64-page document written in Middle English, originally on vellum sheets. In this book, each page contains the same set of couplets, first in modern English (translated by Halliwell), and then in Middle English, so that those who have an interest in the original language can compare the two.

The use of rhyming couplets is a mnemonic device, used in a time when literacy was low, duplication of documents was difficult and slow, and important documents and stories would be memorized, rather than written. Johannes Gutenberg did not invent and use his movable type printing press until 1439, and

William Caxton did not start using the device in England until 1476. Those who could read, even years after the printing press was adopted and widely used, were only those of the higher classes who had the money and time for such education.

Any Mason interested in the history of the Art should read this document and see how it compares to the various rules their grand lodges lay out for government of a lodge.

Carl E. Weaver, Editor
January 2016

I.
Here begin the constitutions of the art of Geometry according to Euclid.
Whoever will both well read and look
He may find written in old book
Of great lords and also ladies,
That had many children together, certainly;
And had no income to keep them with,
Neither in town nor field nor forest;
A council together they could them take,
To ordain for these children's sake,
How they might best lead their life
Without great disease, care and strife;
And most for the multitude that was coming
Of their children, for their success,
They send them to great clerks [scholars],
To teach them then good works;

I.
Hic incipiunt constituciones artis gemetriae secundum Eucyldem.
Whose wol bothe wel rede and loke,
He may fynde wryte yn olde boke,
Of grete lordys and eke ladyysse,
That hade mony chyldryn y-fere, y-wisse;
And hade no rentys to fynde hem wyth,
Nowther yn towne, ny felde, ny fryth:
A cownsel togeder they cowthe hem take;
To ordeyne for these chyldryn sake,
How they mygth best lede here lyfe
Withoute gret desese, care and stryfe;
And most for the multytude that was comynge
Of here chyldryn after here gyndynge.
(They) sende thenne after grete clerkys,
To techyn hem thenne gode werkys;

II.
And pray we them, for our Lord's sake,
To our children some work to make,
That they might get their living thereby,
Both well and honestly full securely.
In that time, through good geometry,
This honest craft of good masonry
Was ordained and made in this manner,
Counterfeited of these clerks together;
At these lord's prayers they counter-feited geometry,
And gave it the name of masonry,
For the most honest craft of all.
These lords' children thereto did fall,
To learn of him the craft of geometry,
The which he made full curiously;

II.
And pray we hem, for our Lordys sake,
To oure chyldryn sum werke to make,
That they mygth gete here lyvynge therby,
Bothe wel and onestlyche, ful sycurly.
Yn that tyme, throggh good gemetry,
Thys onest craft of good masonry
Wes ordeynt and made yn thys manere,
Y-cownterfetyd of thys clerkys y-fere;
At these lordys prayers they cownterfetyd gemetry,
And gaf hyt the name of masonry,
For the moste oneste craft of alle.
These lordys chyldryn therto dede falle,
To lurne of hym the craft of gemetry,
The wheche he made ful curysly;

III.
Through fathers' prayers and mothers' also,
This honest craft he put them to.
He learned best, and was of honesty,
And passed his fellows in curiosity,
If in that craft he did him pass,
He should have more worship than the less,
This great clerk's name was Euclid,
His name it spread full wonder wide.
Yet this great clerk ordained he
To him that was higher in this degree,
That he should teach the simplest of wit
In that honest craft to be perfect;
And so each one shall teach the other,
And love together as sister and brother.

III.
Throggh fadrys prayers and modrys also,
Thys onest craft he putte hem to.
He that lerned best, and were of onesté,
And passud hys felows yn curysté;
[G]ef yn that craft he dede hym passe,
He schulde have more worschepe then the lasse.
Thys grete clerkys name was clept Euclyde,
Hys name hyt spradde ful wondur wyde.
Get thys grete clerke more ordeynt he
To hym that was herre yn thys degré,
That he schulde teche the synplyst of (wytte)
Yn that onest craft to be parfytte;
And so uchon schulle techyn othur,
And love togeder as syster and brothur.

IV.
Futhermore yet that ordained he,
Master called so should he be;
So that he were most worshipped,
Then should he be so called;
But masons should never one another call,
Within the craft amongst them all,
Neither subject nor servant, my dear brother,
Though he be not so perfect as is another;
Each shall call other fellows by friendship,
Because they come of ladies' birth.
On this manner, through good wit of geometry,
Began first the craft of masonry;
The clerk Euclid on this wise it found,
This craft of geometry in Egypt land.

IV.
Forthermore get that ordeynt he,
Mayster y-called so schulde he be;
So that he were most y-worschepede,
Thenne sculde he be so y-clepede:
But mason schulde never won other calle,
Withynne the craft amongus hem alle,
Ny soget, ny servand, my dere brother,
Thaght he be not so perfyt as ys another;
Uchon sculle calle other felows by cuthe,
For cause they come of ladyes burthe.
On thys maner, throg good wytte of gemetry,
Bygan furst the craft of masonry:
The clerk Euclyde on thys wyse hyt fonde,
Thys craft of gemetry yn Egypte londe.

V.
In Egypt he taught it full wide,
In divers lands on every side;
Many years afterwards, I understand,
Ere that the craft came into this land.
This craft came into England, as I to you say,
In time of good King Athelstane's day;
He made then both hall and even bower,
And high temples of great honour,
To disport him in both day and night,
And to worship his God with all his might.
This good lord loved this craft full well,
And purposed to strengthen it every part,
For divers faults that in the craft he found;
He sent about into the land.

V.
Yn Egypte he tawghte hyt ful wyde,
Yn dyvers londe on every syde;
Mony erys afterwarde, y understonde,
[G]er that the craft com ynto thys londe,
Thys craft com ynto Englond, as y gow say,
Yn tyme of good kynge Adelstonus day;
He made tho bothe halle and eke bowre,
And hye templus of gret honowre,
To sportyn hym yn bothe day and nygth,
An to worschepe hys God with alle hys mygth.
Thys goode lorde loved thys craft ful wel,
And purposud to strenthyn hyt every del,
For dyvers defawtys that yn the craft he fonde;
He sende about ynto the londe.

VI.
After all the masons of the craft,
To come to him full even straight,
For to amend these defaults all
By good counsel, if it might fall.
An assembly then could let make
Of divers lords in their state,
Dukes, earls, and barons also,
Knights, squires and many more,
And the great burgesses of that city,
They were there all in their degree;
These were there each one always,
To ordain for these masons' estate,
There they sought by their wit,
How they might govern it:

VI.
After alle the masonus of the crafte,
To come to hym ful evene stragfte,
For to amende these defautys alle
By good consel, gef hyt mytgth falle.
A semblé thenne he cowthe let make
Of dyvers lordis, yn here state,
Dukys, erlys, and barnes also,
yngthys, sqwyers, and mony mo,
And the grete burges of that syté,
They were ther alle yn here degré;
These were ther uchon algate,
To ordeyne for these masonus astate.
Ther they sowgton by here wytte,
How they mygthyn governe hytte:

VII.
Fifteen articles they there sought,
And fifteen points there they wrought,

Here begins the first article.
The first article of this geometry;—
The master mason must be full securely
Both steadfast, trusty and true,
It shall him never then rue;
And pay thy fellows after the cost,
As victuals goeth then, well thou knowest;
And pay them truly, upon thy faith,
What they may deserve;
And to their hire take no more,
But what that they may serve for;
And spare neither for love nor dread,

VII.
Fyftene artyculus they ther sowgton
And fyftene poyntys they wrogton.

Hic incipit articulus primus.
The furste artycul of thys gemetry:—
The mayster mason moste be ful securly
Bothe stedefast, trusty, and trwe,
Hyt schal hum never thenne arewe:
And pay thy felows after the coste,
As vytaylys goth thenne, wel thou woste;
And pay them trwly, apon thy fay,
What that they deserven may;
And to her hure take no more,
But what they mowe serve fore;
And spare, nowther for love ny drede,

VIII.
Of neither parties to take no bribe;
Of lord nor fellow, whoever he be,
Of them thou take no manner of fee;
And as a judge stand upright,
And then thou dost to both good right;
And truly do this wheresoever thou goest,
Thy worship, thy profit, it shall be most.
Second article.
The second article of good masonry,
As you must it here hear specially,
That every master, that is a mason,
Must be at the general congregation,
So that he it reasonably be told
Where that the assembly shall be held;

VIII.
Of nowther partys to take no mede;
Of lord ny felow, whether he be,
Of hem thou take no maner of fe;
And as a jugge stonde uprygth,
And thenne thou dost to bothe good rygth;
And trwly do thys whersever thou gost,
Thy worschep, thy profyt, hyt shcal be most.
Articulus secundus.
The secunde artycul of good masonry,
As ge mowe hyt here hyr specyaly,
That every mayster, that ys a mason,
Most ben at the generale congregacyon,
So that he hyt resonably y-tolde
Where that the semblé schal be holde;

IX.
And to that assembly he must needs gon,
Unless he have a reasonable excuse,
Or unless he be disobedient to that craft,
Or with falsehood is overtaken,
Or else sickness hath him so strong,
That he may not come them among;
That is an excuse good and able,
To that assembly without fable.
Third article.
The third article forsooth it is,
That the master takes to no 'prentice,
Unless he have good assurance to dwell
Seven years with him, as I you tell,
His craft to learn, that is profitable;

IX.
And to that semblé he most nede gon,
But he have a resenabul skwsacyon,
Or but he be unbuxom to that craft,
Or with falssehed ys over-raft,
Or ellus sekenes hath hym so stronge,
That he may not com hem amonge;
That ys a skwsacyon, good and abulle,
To that semblß withoute fabulle.
Articulus tercius.
The thrydde artycul for sothe hyt ysse,
That the mayster take to no prentysse,
but he have good seuerans to dwelle
Seven ger with hym, as y gow telle,
Hys craft to lurne, that ys profytable;

X.
Within less he may no be able
To lords' profit, nor to his own
As you may know by good reason.
Fourth article.
The fourth article this must be,
That the master him well besee,
That he no bondman 'prentice make,
Nor for no covetousness do him take;
For the lord that he is bound to,
May fetch the 'prentice wheresoever he go.
If in the lodge he were taken,
Much disease it might there make,
And such case it might befall,
That it might grieve some or all.

X.
Withynne lasse he may not be able
To lordys profyt, ny to his owne,
As ge mowe knowe by good resowne.
Articulus quartus.
The fowrhe artycul thys moste be
That the mayster hym wel be-se,
That he no bondemon prentys make,
Ny for no covetyse do hym take;
For the lord that he ys bonde to,
May fache the prentes whersever he go.
Gef yn the logge he were y-take,
Muche desese hyt mygth ther make,
And suche case hyt mygth befalle,
That hyt mygth greve summe or alle.

XI.
For all the masons that be there
Will stand together all together.
If such one in that craft should dwell,
Of divers disease you might tell;
For more ease then, and of honesty,
Take a 'prentice of higher degree.
By old time written I find
That the 'prentice should be of gentle kind;
And so sometime, great lords' blood
Took this geometry that is full good.
Fifth article.
The fifth article is very good,
So that the 'prentice be of lawful blood;
The master shall not, for no advantage,

XI.
For alle the masonus tht ben there
Wol stonde togedur hol y-fere
Gef suche won yn that craft schulde swelle,
Of dyvers desesys ge mygth telle:
For more gese thenne, and of honeste,
Take a prentes of herre degre.
By olde tyme wryten y fynde
That the prenes schulde be of gentyl kynde;
And so symtyme grete lordys blod
Toke thys gemetry, that ys ful good.
Articulus quintus.
The fyfthe artycul ys swythe good,
So that the prentes be of lawful blod;
The mayster schal not, for no vantage,

XII.
Make no 'prentice that is deformed;
It is mean, as you may hear,
That he have all his limbs whole all together;
To the craft it were great shame,
To make a halt man and a lame,
For an imperfect man of such blood
Should do the craft but little good.
Thus you may know every one,
The craft would have a mighty man;
A maimed man he hath no might,
You must it know long ere night.
Sixth article.
The sixth article you must not miss,

XII.
Make no prentes that ys outrage;
Hyt ys to mene, as ge mowe here,
That he have hys lymes hole alle y-fere;
To the craft hyt were gret schame,
To make an halt mon and a lame,
For an unperfyt mon of suche blod
Schulde do the craft but lytul good.
Thus ge mowe knowe everychon,
The craft wolde have a myghty mon;
A maymed mon he hath no myght,
[G]e mowe hyt knowe long ger nyght.
Articulus sextus.
The syxte artycul ge mowe not mysse,

XIII.
That the master do the lord no prejudice,
To take the lord for his 'prentice,
As much as his fellows do, in all wise.
For in that craft they be full perfect,
So is not he, you must see it.
Also it were against good reason,
To take his hire as his fellows do.
This same article in this case,
Judgeth his prentice to take less
Than his fellows, that be full perfect.
In divers matters, know requite it,
The master may his 'prentice so inform,
That his hire may increase full soon,

XIII.
That the mayster do the lord no pregedysse,
To take of the lord, for hyse prentyse,
Also muche as hys felows don, yn alle vyse.
For yn that craft they ben ful perfyt,
So ys not he, ge mowe sen hyt.
Also hyt were ageynus good reson,
To take hys, hure as hys felows don.
Thys same artycul, yn thys casse,
Juggythe the prentes to take lasse
Thenne hys felows, that ben ful perfyt.
Yn dyvers maters, conne qwyte hyt,
The mayster may his prentes so enforme,
That hys hure may crese ful gurne,

XIV.
And ere his term come to an end,
His hire may full well amend.
Seventh article.
The seventh article that is now here,
Full well will tell you all together,
That no master for favour nor dread,
Shall no thief neither clothe nor feed.
Thieves he shall harbour never one,
Nor him that hath killed a man,
Nor the same that hath a feeble name,
Lest it would turn the craft to shame.
Eighth article.
The eighth article sheweth you so,

XIV.
And, ger hys terme come to an ende,
Hys hure may ful wel amende.
Articulus septimus.
The seventhe artycul that ys now here,
Ful wel wol telle gow, alle y-fere,
That no mayster, for favour ny drede,
Schal no thef nowther clothe ny fede.
Theves he schal herberon never won,
Ny hym that hath y-quellude a mon,
Wy thylike that hath a febul name,
Lest hyt wolde turne the craft to schame.
Articulus octavus.
The eghte artycul schewt gow so,

XV.
That the master may it well do.
If that he have any man of craft,
And he be not so perfect as he ought,
He may him change soon anon,
And take for him a more perfect man.
Such a man through recklessness,
Might do the craft scant worship.
Ninth article.
The ninth article sheweth full well,
That the master be both wise and strong;
That he no work undertake,
Unless he can both it end and make;
And that it be to the lords' profit also,

XV.
That the mayster may hyt wel do,
[G]ef that he have any mon of crafte,
And be not also perfyt as he augte,
He may hym change sone anon,
And take for hym a perfytur mon.
Suche a mon, throge rechelaschepe,
Mygth do the craft schert worschepe.
Articulus nonus.
The nynthe artycul schewet ful welle,
That the mayster be both wyse and felle;
That no werke he undurtake,
But he conne bothe hyt ende and make;
And that hyt be to the lordes profyt also,

XVI.
And to his craft, wheresoever he go;
And that the ground be well taken,
That it neither flaw nor crack.
Tenth article.
The tenth article is for to know,
Among the craft, to high and low,
There shall no master supplant another,
But be together as sister and brother,
In this curious craft, all and some,
That belongeth to a master mason.
Nor shall he supplant no other man,
That hath taken a work him upon,
In pain thereof that is so strong,

XVI.
And to hys craft, whersever he go;
And that the grond be wel y-take,
That hyt nowther fle ny grake.
Articulus decimus.
The then the artycul ys for to knowe,
Amonge the craft, to hye and lowe,
There schal no mayster supplante other,
But be togeder as systur and brother,
Yn thys curyus craft, alle and som,
That longuth to a maystur mason.
Ny he schal not supplante non other mon,
That hath y-take a werke hym uppon,
Yn peyne therof that ys so stronge,

XVII.
That weigheth no less than ten pounds,
but if that he be guilty found,
That took first the work on hand;
For no man in masonry
Shall not supplant other securely,
But if that it be so wrought,
That in turn the work to nought;
Then may a mason that work crave,
To the lords' profit for it to save
In such a case if it do fall,
There shall no mason meddle withal.
Forsooth he that beginneth the ground,
If he be a mason good and sound,
He hath it securely in his mind

XVII.
That peyseth no lasse thenne ten ponge,
But gef that he be gulty y-fonde,
That toke furst the werke on honde;
For no mon yn masonry
Schal no supplante othur securly,
But gef that hyt be so y-wrogth,
That hyt turne the werke to nogth;
Thenne may a mason that werk crave,
To the lordes profyt hyt for to save;
Yn suche a case but hyt do falle,
Ther schal no mason medul withalle.
Forsothe he that begynnyth the gronde,
And he be a mason goode and sonde,
For hath hyt sycurly yn hys mynde

XVIII.
To bring the work to full good end.
Eleventh article.
The eleventh article I tell thee,
That he is both fair and free;
For he teacheth, by his might,
That no mason should work by night,
But if be in practising of wit,
If that I could amend it.
Twelfth article.
The twelfth article is of high honesty
To every mason wheresoever he be,
He shall not his fellows' work deprave,
If that he will his honesty save;
With honest words he it commend,

XVIII.
To brynge the werke to ful good ende.
Articulus undecimus.
The eleventhe artycul y telle the,
That he ys bothe fayr and fre;
For he techyt, by hys mygth,
That no mason schulde worche be nygth,
But gef hyt be yn practesynge of wytte,
[G]ef that y cowthe amende hytte.
Articulus duodecimus.
The twelfthe artycul ys of hye honesté
To gevery mason, whersever he be;
He schal not hys felows werk deprave,
[G]ef that he wol hys honesté save;
With honest wordes he hyt comende,

XIX.
By the wit God did thee send;
But it amend by all that thou may,
Between you both without doubt.
Thirteenth article.
The thirteenth article, so God me save,
Is if that the master a 'prentice have,
Entirely then that he him teach,
And measurable points that he him tell,
That he the craft ably may know,
Wheresoever he go under the sun.
Fourteenth article.
The fourteenth article by good reason,
Sheweth the master how he shall do;
He shall no 'prentice to him take,

XIX.
By the wytte that God the dede sende;
But hyt amende by al that thou may,
Bytwynne gow bothe withoute nay.
Articulus xiijus.
The threttene artycul, so God me save,
Ys,gef that the mayster a prentes have,
Enterlyche thenne that he hym teche,
And meserable poyntes that he hym reche,
That he the craft abelyche may conne,
Whersever he go undur the sonne.
Articulus xiiijus.
The fowrtene artycul, by good reson,
Scheweth the mayster how he schal don;
He schal no prentes to hym take,

XX.
Unless diver cares he have to make,
That he may within his term,
Of him divers points may learn.
Fifteenth article.
The fifteenth article maketh an end,
For to the master he is a friend;
To teach him so, that for no man,
No false maintenance he take him upon,
Nor maintain his fellows in their sin,
For no good that he might win;
Nor no false oath suffer him to make,
For dread of their souls' sake,
Lest it would turn the craft to shame,
And himself to very much blame.

XX.
Byt dyvers crys he have to make,
That he may, withynne hys terme,
Of hym dyvers poyntes may lurne.
Articulus quindecimus.
The fyftene artycul maketh an ende,
For to the mayster he ys a frende;
To lere hym so, that for no mon,
No fals mantenans he take hym apon,
Ny maynteine hys felows yn here synne,
For no good that he mygth wynne;
Ny no fals sware sofre hem to make,
For drede of here sowles sake;
Lest hyt wolde turne the craft to schame,
And hymself to mechul blame.

XXI.
Plural constitutions.
At this assembly were points ordained more,
Of great lords and masters also.
That who will know this craft and come to estate,
He must love well God and holy church always,
And his master also that he is with,
Whersoever he go in field or enclosed wood,
And thy fellows thou love also,
For that thy craft will that thou do.
Second Point.
The second point as I you say,
That the mason work upon the work day,
As truly as he can or may,

XXI.
Plures Constituciones.
At thys semblé were poyntes y-ordeynt mo,
Of grete lordys and maystrys also,
That whose wol conne thys craft and com to astate,
He most love wel God, and holy churche algate,
And hys mayster also, that he ys wythe,
Whersever he go, yn fylde or frythe;
And thy felows thou love also,
For that they craft wol that thou do.
Secundus punctus.
The secunde poynt, as y gow say,
That the mason worche apon the werk day,
Also trwly, as he con or may,

XXII.
To deserve his hire for the holy-day,
And truly to labour on his deed,
Well deserve to have his reward.
Third Point.
The third point must be severely,
With the 'prentice know it well,
His master's counsel he keep and close,
And his fellows by his good purpose;
The privities of the chamber tell he no man,
Nor in the lodge whatsoever they do;
Whatsoever thou hearest or seest them do,
Tell it no man wheresoever you go;
The counsel of hall, and even of bower,

XXII.
To deserve hys huyre for the halyday,
And trwly to labrun on hys dede,
Wel deserve to have hys mede.
Tercius punctus.
The thrydde poynt most be severele,
With the prentes knowe hyt wele,
Hys mayster conwsel he kepe and close,
And hys felows by hys goode purpose;
The prevetyse of the chamber telle he no man,
Ny yn the logge whatsever they done;
Whatsever thou heryst, or syste hem do,
Telle hyt no mon, whersever thou go;
The conwsel of halls, and geke of bowre,

XXIII.
Keep it well to great honour,
Lest it would turn thyself to blame,
And bring the craft into great shame.
Fourth Point.
The fourth point teacheth us also,
That no man to his craft be false;
Error he shall maintain none
Against the craft, but let it go;
Nor no prejudice he shall no do
To his master, nor his fellow also;
And though the 'prentice be under awe,
Yet he would have the same law.

XXIII.
Kepe hyt wel to gret honowre,
Lest hyt wolde torne thyself to blame,
And brynge the craft ynto gret schame.
Quartus punctus.
The fowrthe poynt techyth us alse,
That no mon to hys craft be false;
Errour he schal maynteine none
Ageynus the craft, but let hyt gone;
Ny no pregedysse he schal not do
To hys mayster, ny hys felows also;
And thatgth the prentes be under awe,
[G]et he wolde have the same lawe.

XXIV.
Fifth Point.
The fifth point is without doubt,
That when the mason taketh his pay
Of the master, ordained to him,
Full meekly taken so must it be;
Yet must the master by good reason,
Warn him lawfully before noon,
If he will not occupy him no more,
As he hath done there before;
Against this order he may no strive,
If he think well for to thrive.
Sixth Point.
The sixth point is full given to know,
Both to high and even low,

XXIV.
Quintus punctus.
The fyfthe poynte ys, withoute nay,
That whenne the mason taketh hys pay
Of the mayster, y-ordent to hym,
Ful mekely y-take so most hyt byn;
[G]et most the mayster, by good resone,
Warne hem lawfully byfore none,
[G]ef he nulle okepye hem no more,
As he hath y-done ther byfore;
Ageynus thys ordyr he may not stryve,
[G]ef he thenke wel for to thryve.
Sextus punctus.
The syxte poynt ys ful gef to knowe,
Bothe to hye and eke to lowe,

XXV.
For such case it might befall;
Among the masons some or all,
Through envy or deadly hate,
Oft ariseth full great debate.
Then ought the mason if that he may,
Put them both under a day;
But loveday yet shall they make none,
Till that the work-day be clean gone
Upon the holy-day you must well take,
Leisure enough loveday to make,
Lest that it would the work-day
Hinder their work for such a fray;
To such end then that you them draw.

XXV.
For suche case hyt mygth befalle,
Amonge the masonus, summe or alle,
Throwghe envye, or dedly hate,
Ofte aryseth ful gret debate.
Thenne owyth the mason, gef that he may,
Putte hem bothe under a day;
But loveday get schul they make none;
Tyl that the werke day be clene a-gone;
Apon the holyday ge mowe wel take
Leyser y-nowggth loveday to make,
Lest that hyt wolde the werke day
Latte here werke for suche afray;
To suche ende thenne that hem drawe,

XXVI.
That they stand well in God's law.
Seventh Point.
The seventh point he may well mean,
Of well long life that God us lend,
As it descrieth well openly,
Thou shalt not by thy master's wife lie,
Nor by thy fellows', in no manner wise,
Lest the craft would thee despise;
Nor by thy fellows' concubine,
No more thou wouldst he did by thine.
The pain thereof let it be sure,
That he be 'prentice full seven year,
If he forfeit in any of them,

XXVI.
That they stonde wel yn Goddes lawe.
Septimus punctus.
The seventhe poynt he may wel mene,
Of wel longe lyf that God us lene,
As hyt dyscryeth wel opunly,
Thou schal not by thy maysters wyf ly,
Ny by the felows, yn no maner wyse,
Lest the craft wolde the despyse;
Ny by the felows concubyne,
No more thou woldest he dede by thyne.
The peyne thereof let hyt be ser,
That he prentes ful seven ger,
[G]ef he forfete yn eny of hem,

XXVII.
So chastised then must he be;
Full much care might there begin,
For such a foul deadly sin.
Eighth Point.
The eighth point, he may be sure,
If thou hast taken any cure,
Under thy master thou be true,
For that point thous shalt never rue;
A true mediator thou must needs be
To thy master, and thy fellows free;
Do truly all that thou might,
To both parties, and that is good right.

XXVII.
So y-chasted thenne most he ben;
Ful mekele care mygth ther begynne,
For suche a fowle dedely synne.
Octavus punctus.
The eghte poynt, he may be sure,
[G]ef thou hast y-taken any cure,
Under thy mayster thou be trwe,
For that pynt thou schalt never arewe;
A trwe medyater thou most nede be
To thy mayster, and thy felows fre;
Do trwly al....that thou mygth,
To both partyes, and that ys good rygth.

XXVIII.
Ninth Point.
The ninth point we shall him call,
That he be steward of our hall,
If that you be in chamber together,
Each one serve other with mild cheer;
Gentle fellows, you must it know,
For to be stewards all in turn,
Week after week without doubt,
Stewards to be so all in turn about,
Amiably to serve each one other,
As though they were sister and brother;
There shall never one another cost
Free himself to no advantage,
But every man shall be equally free

XXVIII.
Nonus punctus.
The nynthe poynt we schul hym calle,
That he be stwarde of oure halle,
Gef that ge ben yn chambur y-fere,
Uchon serve other, with mylde chere;
Jentul felows, ge moste hyt knowe,
For to be stwardus alle o rowe,
Weke after weke withoute dowte,
Stwardus to ben so alle abowte,
Lovelyche to serven uchon othur,
As thawgh they were syster and brother;
Ther schal never won on other costage
Fre hymself to no vantage,
But every mon schal be lyche fre

XXIX.
In that cost, so must it be;
Look that thou pay well every man always,
That thou hast bought any victuals eaten,
That no craving be made to thee,
Nor to thy fellows in no degree,
To man or to woman, whoever he be,
Pay them well and truly, for that will we;
Therof on thy fellow true record thou take,
For that good pay as thou dost make,
Lest it would thy fellow shame,
And bring thyself into great blame.
Yet good accounts he must make
Of such goods as he hath taken,

XXIX.
Yn that costage, so moste hyt be;
Loke that thou pay wele every mon algate,
That thou hsat y-bowght any vytayles ate,
That no cravynge be y-mad to the,
Ny to thy felows, yn no degré,
To mon or to wommon, whether he be,
Pay hem wel and trwly, for that wol we;
Therof on thy felow trwe record thou take,
For that good pay as thou dost make,
Lest hyt wolde thy felowe schame,
Any brynge thyself ynto gret blame.
[G]et good acowntes he most make
Of suche godes as he hath y-take,

XXX.
Of thy fellows' goods that thou hast spent,
Where and how and to what end;
Such accounts thou must come to,
When thy fellows wish that thou do.
Tenth Point.
The tenth point presenteth well good life,
To live without care and strife;
For if the mason live amiss,
And in his work be false I know,
And through such a false excuse
May slander his fellows without reason,
Through false slander of such fame

XXX.
Of thy felows goodes that thou hast spende,
Wher, and how, and to what ende;
Suche acowntes thou most come to,
Whenne thy felows wollen that thou do.
Decimus punctus.
The tenthe poynt presentyeth wel god lyf,
To lyven withoute care and stryf;
For and the mason lyve amysse,
And yn hys werk be false, y-wysse,
And thorwg suche a false skewysasyon
May sclawndren hys felows oute reson,
Throwg false sclawnder of suche fame

XXXI.
May make the craft acquire blame.
If he do the craft such villainy,
Do him no favour then securely,
Nor maintain not him in wicked life,
Lest it would turn to care and strife;
But yet him you shall not delay,
Unless that you shall him constrain,
For to appear wheresoever you will,
Where that you will, loud, or still;
To the next assembly you him call,
To appear before his fellows all,
And unless he will before them appear,

XXXI.
May make the craft kachone blame.
[G]ef he do the craft suche vylany,
Do hym no favour thenne securly.
Ny maynteine not hym yn wyked lyf,
Lest hyt wolde turne to care and stryf;
But get hym ge schul not delayme,
But that ge schullen hym constrayne,
For to apere whersevor ge wylle,
Whar that ge wolen, lowde, or stylle;
To the nexte semblß ge schul hym calle,
To apere byfore hys felows alle,
And but gef he wyl byfore hem pere,

XXXII.
The craft he must need forswear;
He shall then be punished after the law
That was founded by old day.
Eleventh Point.
The eleventh point is of good discretion,
As you must know by good reason;
A mason, if he this craft well know,
That seeth his fellow hew on a stone,
And is in point to spoil that stone,
Amend it soon if that thou can,
And teach him then it to amend,
That the lords' work be not spoiled,
And teach him easily it to amend,

XXXII.
The crafte he moste nede forswere;
He schal thenne be chasted after the lawe
That was y-fownded by olde dawe.
Punctus undecimus.
The eleventhe poynt ys of good dyscrecyoun,
As ge mowe knowe by good resoun;
A mason, and he thys craft wel con,
That sygth hys felow hewen on a ston,
And ys yn poynt to spylle that ston,
Amende hyt sone, gef that thou con,
And teche hym thenne hyt to amende,
That the l(ordys) werke be not y-schende,
And teche hym esely hyt to amende,

XXXIII.
With fair words, that God thee hath lent;
For his sake that sit above,
With sweet words nourish his love.
Twelfth Point.
The twelfth point is of great royalty,
There as the assembly held shall be,
There shall be masters and fellows also,
And other great lords many more;
There shall be the sheriff of that country,
And also the mayor of that city,
Knights and squires there shall be,
And also aldermen, as you shall see;
Such ordinance as they make there,

XXXIII.
With fayre wordes, that God the hath lende;
For hys sake that sytte above,
With swete wordes noresche hym love.
Punctus duodecimus.
The twelthe poynt of gret ryolté,
Ther as the semblß y-hole schal be,
Ther schul be maystrys and felows also,
And other grete lordes mony mo;
There schal be the scheref of that contré,
And also the meyr of that syté,
Knygtes and sqwyers ther schul be,
And other aldermen, as ge schul se;
Suche ordynance as they maken there,

XXXIV.
They shall maintain it all together
Against that man, whatsoever he be,
That belongeth to the craft both fair and free.
If he any strife against them make,
Into their custody he shall be taken.
Thirteenth Point.
The thirteenth point is to us full lief,
He shall swear never to be no thief,
Nor succour him in his false craft,
For no good that he hath bereft,
And thou must it know or sin,
Neither for his good, nor for his kin.

XXXIV.
They schul mayntß hyt hol y-fere
Ageynus that mon, whatsever he be,
That longuth to the craft bothe fayr and fre.
[G]ef he any stryf ageynus hem make,
Ynto here warde he schal be take.
Xiijus punctus.
The threnteth poynt ys to us ful luf.
He schal swere never to be no thef,
Ny soker hym yn hys fals craft,
For no good that he hath byraft,
And thou mowe hyt knowe or syn,
Nowther for hys good, ny for hys kyn.

XXXV.
Fourteenth Point.
The fourteenth point is full good law
To him that would be under awe;
A good true oath he must there swear
To his master and his fellows that be there;
He must be steadfast be and true also
To all this ordinance, wheresoever he go,
And to his liege lord the king,
To be true to him over all thing.
And all these points here before
To them thou must need be sworn,
And all shall swear the same oath
Of the masons, be they lief be they loath.
To all these points here before,

XXXV.
Xiiijus punctus.
The fowrtethe poynt ys ful good lawe
To hym that wold ben under awe;
A good trwe othe he most ther swere
To hys mayster and hys felows that ben there;
He most be stedefast and trwe also
To alle thys ordynance, whersever he go,
And to hys lyge lord the kynge,
To be trwe to hym, over alle thynge.
And alle these poyntes hyr before
To hem thou most nede by y-swore,
And alle schul swere the same ogth
Of the masonus, be they luf, ben they loght,
To alle these poyntes hyr byfore,

XXXVI.
That hath been ordained by full good lore.
And they shall enquire every man
Of his party, as well as he can,
If any man may be found guilty
In any of these points specially;
And who he be, let him be sought,
And to the assembly let him be brought.
Fifteen Point.
The fifteenth point is full good lore,
For them that shall be there sworn,
Such ordinance at the assembly was laid
Of great lords and masters before said;
For the same that be disobedient, I know,

XXXVI.
That hath ben ordeynt by ful good lore.
And they schul enquere every mon
On his party, as wyl as he con,
[G]ef any mon mowe be y-fownde gulty
Yn any of these poyntes spesyaly;
And whad he be, let hym be sowght,
And to the semblß let hym be browght.
Quindecimus punctus.
The fifethe poynt ys of ful good lore,
For hem that schul ben ther y-swore,
Suche ordyance at the semblß wes layd
Of grete lordes and maystres byforesayd;
For thelke that be unbuxom, y-wysse,

XXXVII.
Against the ordinance that there is,
Of these articles that were moved there,
Of great lords and masons all together,
And if they be proved openly
Before that assembly, by and by,
And for their guilt's no amends will make,
Then must they need the craft forsake;
And no masons craft they shall refuse,
And swear it never more to use.
But if that they will amends make,
Again to the craft they shall never take;
And if that they will no do so,
The sheriff shall come them soon to,

XXXVII.
Ageynus the ordynance that ther ysse
Of these artyculus, that were y-meved there,
Of grete lordes and masonus al y-fere.
And gef they ben y-preved opunly
Byfore that semblß, by an by,
And for here gultes no mendys wol make,
Thenne most they nede the craft forsake;
And so masonus craft they schul refuse,
And swere hyt never more for to use.
But gef that they wol mendys make,
Agayn to the craft they schul never take;
And gef that they nul not do so,
The scheref schal come hem sone to,

XXXVIII.
And put their bodies in deep prison,
For the trespass that they have done,
And take their goods and their cattle
Into the king's hand, every part,
And let them dwell there full still,
Till it be our liege king's will.
Another ordinance of the art of geometry.
They ordained there an assembly to be hold,
Every year, wheresoever they would,
To amend the defaults, if any were found
Among the craft within the land;
Each year or third year it should be held,

XXXVIII.
And putte here bodyes yn duppe prison,
For the trespasse that they hav y-don,
And take here goodes and here cattelle
Ynto the kynges hond, everyt delle,
And lete hem dwelle ther full stylle,
Tyl hyt be oure lege kynges wylle.
Alia ordinacio artis gematriae.
They ordent ther a semblé to be y-holde
Every ger, whersever they wolde,
To amende the defautes, gef any where fonde
Amonge the craft withynne the londe;
Uche ger or thrydde ger hyt schuld be holde,

XXXIX.
In every place weresoever they would;
Time and place must be ordained also,
In what place they should assemble to,
All the men of craft there they must be,
And other great lords, as you must see,
To mend the faults the he there spoken,
If that any of them be then broken.
There they shall be all sworn,
That belongeth to this craft's lore,
To keep their statutes every one
That were ordained by King Althelstane;
These statutes that I have here found

XXXIX.
Yn every place whersever they wolde;
Tyme and place most be ordeynt also,
Yn what place they schul semble to.
Alle the men of craft tehr they most ben,
And other grete lordes, as ge mowe sen,
To mende the fautes that buth ther y-spoke,
[G]ef that eny of hem ben thenne y-broke.
Ther they schullen ben alle y-swore,
That longuth to thys craftes lore,
To kepe these statutes everychon,
That ben y-ordeynt by kynge Aldelston;
These statutes that y have hyr y-fonde

XL.
I ordain they be held through my land,
For the worship of my royalty,
That I have by my dignity.
Also at every assembly that you hold,
That you come to your liege king bold,
Beseeching him of his grace,
To stand with you in every place,
To confirm the statutes of King Athelstane,
That he ordained to this craft by good reason.
The art of the four crowned ones .
Pray we now to God almighty,
And to his mother Mary bright,

XL.
Y chulle they ben holde throgh my londe,
For the worsche of my rygolté,
That y have by my dygnyté.
Also at every semblé that ge holde,
That ge come to gowre lyge kyng bolde,
Bysechynge hym of hys hye grace,
To stonde with gow yn every place,
To conferme the statutes of kynge Adelston,
That he ordeydnt to thys craft by good reson.
Ars quatuor coronatorum.
Pray we now to God almyght,
And to hys moder Mary bryght,

XLI.

That we may keep these articles here,
And these points well all together,
As did these holy martyrs four,
That in this craft were of great honour;
They were as good masons as on earth shall go,
Gravers and image-makers they were also.
For they were workmen of the best,
The emperor had to them great liking;
He willed of them an image to make
That might be worshipped for his sake;
Such monuments he had in his day,
To turn the people from Christ's law.

XLI.

That we mowe keepe these artyculus here,
And these poynts wel al y-fere,
As dede these holy martyres fowre,
That yn thys craft were of gret honoure;
They were as gode masonus as on erthe schul go,
Gravers and ymage-makers they were also.
For they were werkemen of the beste,
The emperour hade to hem gret luste;
He wylned of hem a ymage to make,
That mowgh be worscheped for his sake;
Suche mawmetys he hade yn hys dawe,
To turne the pepul from Crystus lawe.

XLII.
But they were steadfast in Christ's law,
And to their craft without doubt;
They loved well God and all his lore,
And were in his service ever more.
True men they were in that day,
And lived well in God's law;
They thought no monuments for to make,
For no good that they might take,
To believe on that monument for their God,
They would not do so, though he was furious;
For they would not forsake their true faith,

XLII.
But they were stedefast yn Crystes lay,
And to here craft, withouten nay;
They loved wel God and alle hys lore,
And weren yn hys serves ever more.
Trwe men they were yn that dawe,
And lyved wel y Goddus lawe;
They thogght no mawmetys for to make,
For no good that they mygth take,
To levyn on that mawmetys for here God,
They nolde do so thawg he were wod;
For they nolde not forsake here trw fay,

XLIII.
And believe on his false law,
The emperor let take them soon anon,
And put them in a deep prison;
The more sorely he punished them in that place,
The more joy was to them of Christ's grace,
Then when he saw no other one,
To death he let them then go;
Whose will of their life yet more know
By the book he might it show
In legend of holy ones,
The names of the four-crowned ones.

XLIII.
An beyleve on hys falsse lay.
The emperour let take hem sone anone,
And putte hem ynto a dep presone;
The sarre he penest hem yn that plase,
The more yoye wes to hem of Cristus grace.
Thenne when he sye no nother won,
To dethe he lette hem thenne gon;
Whose wol of here lyf get mor knowe,
By the bok he may kyt schowe,
In the legent of scanctorum,
The name of quatour coronatorum.

XLIV.
Their feast will be without doubt,
After Hallow-e'en eighth day.
You may hear as I do read,
That many years after, for great dread
That Noah's flood was all run,
The tower of Babylon was begun,
As plain work of lime and stone,
As any man should look upon;
So long and broad it was begun,
Seven miles the height shadoweth the sun.
King Nebuchadnezzar let it make
To great strength for man's sake,

XLIV.
Here fest wol be, withoute nay,
After Alle Halwen the eyght day.
[G]e mow here as y do rede,
That mony geres after, for gret drede
That Noees flod wes alle y-ronne,
The tower of Babyloyne was begonne,
Also playne werke of lyme and ston,
As any mon schulde loke uppon;
So long and brod hyt was begonne,
Seven myle the hegghte schadweth the sonne.
King Nabogodonosor let hyt make,
To gret strenthe for monus sake,

XLV.
Though such a flood again should come,
Over the work it should not take;
For they had so high pride, with strong boast
All that work therefore was lost;
An angel smote them so with divers speech,
That never one knew what the other should tell.
Many years after, the good clerk Euclid
Taught the craft of geometry full wonder wide,
So he did that other time also,
Of divers crafts many more.
Through high grace of Christ in heaven,
He commenced in the sciences seven;

XLV.
Thaggh suche a flod agayne schulde come,
Over the werke hyt schulde not nome;
For they hadde so hy pride, with stronge bost,
Alle that werke therfore was y-lost;
An angele smot hem so with dyveres speche,
That never won wyste what other schuld reche.
Mony eres after, the goode clerk Euclyde
Tagghte the craft of gemetrß wonder wyde,
So he ded that tyme other also,
Of dyvers craftes mony mo.
Throggh hye grace of Crist yn heven,
He commensed yn the syens seven;

XLVI.
Grammar is the first science I know,
Dialect the second, so I have I bliss,
Rhetoric the third without doubt,
Music is the fourth, as I you say,
Astronomy is the fifth, by my snout,
Arithmetic the sixth, without doubt,
Geometry the seventh maketh an end,
For he is both meek and courteous,
Grammar forsooth is the root,
Whoever will learn on the book;
But art passeth in his degree,
As the fruit doth the root of the tree;

XLVI.
Gramatica ys the furste syens y-wysse,
Dialetica the secunde, so have y blysse,
Rethorica the thrydde, withoute nay,
Musica ys the fowrth, as y gow say,
Astromia ys the v, by my snowte,
Arsmetica the vi, withoute dowte
Gemetria the seventhe maketh an ende,
For he ys bothe make and hende,
Gramer forsothe ys the rote,
Whose wyl lurne on the boke;
But art passeth yn hys degré,
As the fryte doth the rote of the tre;

XLVII.
Rhetoric measureth with ornate speech among,
And music it is a sweet song;
Astronomy numbereth, my dear brother,
Arithmetic sheweth one thing that is another,
Geometry the seventh science it is,
That can separate falsehood from truth, I know
These be the sciences seven,
Who useth them well he may have heaven.
Now dear children by your wit
Pride and covetousness that you leave it,
And taketh heed to good discretion,
And to good nurture, wheresoever you come.
Now I pray you take good heed,

XLVII.
Rethoryk metryth with orne speche amonge,
And musyke hyt ys a swete song;
Astronomy nombreth, my dere brother,
Arsmetyk scheweth won thyng that ys another,
Gemetrß the seventh syens hyt ysse,
That con deperte falshed from trewthe y-wys.
These bene the syens seven,
Whose useth hem wel, he may han heven.
Now dere chyldren, by gowre wytte,
Pride and covetyse that ge leven, hytte,
And taketh hede to goode dyscrecyon,
And to good norter, whersever ge com.
Now y pray gow take good hede,

XLVIII.
For this you must know needs,
But much more you must know,
Than you find here written.
If thee fail therto wit,
Pray to God to send thee it;
For Christ himself, he teacheth us
That holy church is God's house,
That is made for nothing else
But for to pray in, as the book tells us;
There the people shall gather in,
To pray and weep for their sin.
Look thou come not to church late,
For to speak harlotry by the gate;

XLVIII.
For thys ge most kenne nede,
But much more ge moste wyten,
Thenne ge fynden hyr y-wryten.
[G]ef the fayle therto wytte,
Pray to God to send the hytte;
For Crist hymself, he techet ous
That holy churche ys Goddes hous,
That ys y-mad for nothynge ellus
but for to pray yn, as the bok tellus;
Ther the pepul schal gedur ynne,
To pray and wepe for here synne.
Loke thou come not to churche late,
For to speke harlotry by the gate;

XLIX.
Then to church when thou dost fare,
Have in thy mind ever more
To worship thy lord God both day and night,
With all thy wits and even thy might.
To the church door when thou dost come
Of that holy water there some thou take,
For every drop thou feelest there
Quencheth a venial sin, be thou sure.
But first thou must do down thy hood,
For his love that died on the rood.
Into the church when thou dost go,
Pull up thy heart to Christ, anon [presently];

XLIX.
Thenne to churche when thou dost fare,
Have yn thy mynde ever mare
To worschepe thy lord God bothe day and nygth,
With all thy wyttes, and eke thy mygth.
To the churche dore when tou dost come,
Of that holy water ther sum thow nome,
For every drope thou felust ther
Qwenchet a venyal synne, be thou ser.
But furst thou most do down thy hode,
For hyse love that dyed on the rode.
Into the churche when thou dost gon,
Pulle uppe thy herte to Crist, anon;

L.
Upon the rood thou look up then,
And kneel down fair upon thy knees,
Then pray to him so here to work,
After the law of holy church,
For to keep the commandments ten,
That God gave to all men;
And pray to him with mild voice
To keep thee from the sins seven,
That thou here may, in this life,
Keep thee well from care and strife;
Furthermore he grant thee grace,
In heaven's bliss to have a place.

L.
Uppon the rode thou loke uppe then,
And knele down fayre on bothe thy knen;
Then pray to hym so hyr to worche,
After the lawe of holy churche,
For to kepe the comandementes ten,
That God gaf to alle men;
And pray to hym with mylde steven
To kepe the from the synnes seven,
That thou hyr mowe, yn thy lyve,
Kepe the wel from care and stryve,
Forthermore he grante the grace,
In heven blysse to hav a place.

LI.
In holy churche lef nyse wordes
Of lewed speche, and fowle bordes,
And putte away alle vanyté,
And say thy pater noster and thyn ave;
Loke also thou make no bere,
But ay to be yn thy prayere;
[G]ef thou wolt not thyselve pray,
Latte non other mon by no way.
In that place nowther sytte ny stonde,
But knele fayre down on the gronde,
And, when the Gospel me rede schal,

LI.
In holy church leave trifling words
Of lewd speech and foul jests,
And put away all vanity,
And say thy pater noster and thine ave;
Look also that thou make no noise,
But always to be in thy prayer;
If thou wilt not thyself pray,
Hinder no other man by no way.
In that place neither sit nor stand,
But kneel fair down on the ground,
And when the Gospel me read shall,

LII.
Fairly thou stand up from the wall,
And bless the fare if that thou can,
When gloria tibi is begun;
And when the gospel is done,
Again thou might kneel down,
On both knees down thou fall,
For his love that bought us all;
And when thou hearest the bell ring
To that holy sacrament,
Kneel you must both young and old,
And both your hands fair uphold,
And say then in this manner,

LII.
Fayre thou stonde up fro the wal,
And blesse the fayre, gef that thou conne,
When gloria tibi is begonne;
And when the gospel ys y-done,
Agayn thou mygth knele adown;
On bothe thy knen down thou falle,
For hyse love that bowght us alle;
And when thou herest the belle rynge
To that holy sakerynge,
Knele ge most, bothe gynge and olde,
And bothe gor hondes fayr upholde,
And say thenne yn thys manere,

LIII.
Fair and soft without noise;
"Jesu Lord welcome thou be,
In form of bread as I thee see,
Now Jesu for thine holy name,
Shield me from sin and shame;
Shrift and Eucharist thou grand me both,
Ere that I shall hence go,
And very contrition for my sin,
That I never, Lord, die therein;
And as thou were of maid born,
Suffer me never to be lost;
But when I shall hence wend,

LIII.
Fayr and softe, withoute bere;
"Jhesu Lord, welcom thou be,
Yn forme of bred, as y the se.
Now Jhesu, for thyn holy name,
Schulde me from synne and schame,
Schryff and hosel thou grant me bo,
[G]er that y schal hennus go,
And vey contrycyon of my synne,
Tath y never, Lord, dye therynne;
And, as thou were of a mayde y-bore,
Sofre me never to be y-lore;
But when y schal hennus wende,

LIV.
Grant me the bliss without end;
Amen! Amen! so mote it be!
Now sweet lady pray for me."
Thus thou might say, or some other thing,
When thou kneelest at the sacrament.
For covetousness after good, spare thou not
To worship him that all hath wrought;
For glad may a man that day be,
That once in the day may him see;
It is so much worth, without doubt,
The virtue thereof no man tell may;
But so much good doth that sight,

LIV.
Grante me the blysse withoute ende;
Amen! amen! so mot hyt be!
Now, swete lady, pray for me."
Thus thou myght say, or sum other thynge,
When thou knelust at the sakerynge.
For covetyse after good, spare thou nought
To worschepe hym that alle hath wrought;
For glad may a mon that day ben,
That onus yn the day may hym sen;
Hyt ys so muche worthe, withoute nay,
The vertu therof no mon telle may;
But so meche good doth that syht,

LV.
That Saint Austin telleth full right,
That day thou seest God's body,
Thou shalt have these full securely:—
Meet and drink at thy need,
None that day shalt thou lack;
Idle oaths and words both,
God forgiveth thee also;
Sudden death that same day
Thee dare not dread by no way;
Also that day, I thee plight,
Thou shalt not lose thy eye sight;
And each foot that thou goest then,

LV.
As seynt Austyn telluth ful ryht,
That day thou syst Goddus body,
Thou schalt have these, ful securly:—
Mete and drynke at thy nede,
Non that day schal the gnede;
Ydul othes, an wordes bo,
God forgeveth the also;
Soden deth, that ylke day,
The dar not drede by no way;
Also that day, y the plyht,
Thou schalt not lese thy eye syht;
And uche fote that thou gost then,

LVI.
That holy sight for to see,
They shall be told to stand instead,
When thou hast thereto great need;
That messenger the angel Gabriel,
Will keep them to thee full well.
From this matter now I may pass,
To tell more benefits of the mass:
To church come yet, if thou may,
And hear the mass each day;
If thou may not come to church,
Where that ever thou dost work,
When thou hearest the mass toll,

LVI.
That holy syht for to sen,
They schul be told to stonde yn stede,
When thou hast therto gret nede;
That messongere, the angele Gabryelle,
Wol kepe hem to the ful welle.
From thys mater now y may passe,
To telle mo medys of the masse:
To churche come get, gef thou may,
And here thy masse uche day;
[G]ef thou mowe not come to churche,
Wher that ever thou doste worche,
When thou herest to masse knylle,

LVII.
Pray to God with heart still,
To give thy part of that service,
That in church there done is.
Furthermore yet, I will you preach
To your fellows, it for to teach,
When thou comest before a lord,
In hall, in bower, or at the board,
Hood or cap that thou off do,
Ere thou come him entirely to;
Twice or thrice, without doubt,
To that lord thou must bow;
With thy right knee let it be done,

LVII.
Pray to God with herte stylle,
To geve the part of that servyse,
That yn churche ther don yse.
Forthermore get, y wol gow preche
To gowre felows, hyt for to teche,
When thou comest byfore a lorde,
Yn halle, yn bowre, or at the borde,
Hod or cappe that thou of do,
[G]er thou come hym allynge to;
Twyes or thryes, without dowte,
To that lord thou moste lowte;
With thy rygth kne let hyt be do,

LVIII.
Thine own worship thou save so.
Hold off thy cap and hood also,
Till thou have leave it on to put.
All the time thou speakest with him,
Fair and amiably hold up thy chin;
So after the nurture of the book,
In his face kindly thou look.
Foot and hand thou keep full still,
For clawing and tripping, is skill;
From spitting and sniffling keep thee also,
By private expulsion let it go,
And if that thou be wise and discrete,

LVIII.
Thyn owne worschepe tou save so.
Holde of thy cappe, and hod also,
Tyl thou have leve hyt on to do.
Al the whyle thou spekest with hym,
Fayre and lovelyche bere up thy chyn;
So, after the norter of the boke,
Yn hys face lovely thou loke.
Fot and hond, thou kepe ful stylle
From clawynge and trypynge, ys sckylle;
From spyttynge and snyftynge kepe the also,
By privy avoydans let hyt go.
And gef that thou be wyse and felle,

LIX.
Thou has great need to govern thee well.
Into the hall when thou dost wend,
Amongst the gentles, good and courteous,
Presume not too high for nothing,
For thine high blood, nor thy cunning,
Neither to sit nor to lean,
That is nurture good and clean.
Let not thy countenance therefor abate,
Forsooth good nurture will save thy state.
Father and mother, whatsoever they be,
Well is the child that well may thee,
In hall, in chamber, where thou dost go;

LIX.
Thou hast gret nede to governe the welle.
Ynto the halle when thou dost wende,
Amonges the genteles, good and hende,
Presume not to hye for nothynge,
For thyn hye blod, ny thy connynge,
Nowther to sytte, ny to lene,
That ys norther good and clene.
Let not thy cowntenans therfore abate,
Forsothe, good norter wol save thy state.
Fader and moder, whatsever they be,
Wel ys the chyld that wel may the,
Yn halle, yn chamber, wher thou dost gon;

LX.
Good manners make a man.
To the next degree look wisely,
To do them reverence by and by;
Do them yet no reverence all in turn,
Unless that thou do them know.
To the meat when thou art set,
Fair and honestly thou eat it;
First look that thine hands be clean,
And that thy knife be sharp and keen,
And cut thy bread all at thy meat,
Right as it may be there eaten,
If thou sit by a worthier man,

LX.
Gode maneres maken a mon.
To the nexte degrß loke wysly,
To do hem reverans by and by;
Do hem get no reverans al o-rowe,
But gef that thou do hem know.
To the mete when thou art y-sette,
Fayre and onestelyche thou ete hytte;
Fyrst loke that thyn honden be clene,
And that thy knyf be scharpe and kene;
And kette thy bred al at thy mete,
Rygth as hyt may be ther y-ete.
[G]ef thou sytte by a worththyur mon.

LXI.
Then thy self thou art one,
Suffer him first to touch the meat,
Ere thyself to it reach.
To the fairest morsel thou might not strike,
Though that thou do it well like;
Keep thine hands fair and well,
From foul smudging of thy towel;
Thereon thou shalt not thy nose blow,
Nor at the meat thy tooth thou pick;
Too deep in cup thou might not sink,
Though thou have good will to drink,
Lest thine eyes would water thereby —

LXI.
Then thy selven thou art won,
Sofre hym fyrst to toyche the mete,
[G]er thyself to hyt reche.
To the fayrest mossel thou myght not strike,
Thaght that thou do hyt wel lyke;
Kepe thyn hondes, fayr and wel,
From fowle smogynge of thy towel;
Theron thou schalt not thy nese snyte,
Ny at the mete thy tothe thou pyke;
To depe yn the coppe thou mygght not synke,
Thagh thou have good wyl to drynke,
Lest thyn enyn wolde wattryn therby—

LXII.
Then were it no courtesy.
Look in thy mouth there be no meat,
When thou begins to drink or speak.
When thou seest any man drinking,
That taketh heed to thy speech,
Soon anaon thou cease thy tale,
Whether he drink wine or ale,
Look also thou scorn no man,
In what degree thou seest him gone;
Nor thou shalt no man deprave,
If thou wilt thy worship save;
For such word might there outburst.

LXII.
Then were hyt no curtesy
Loke yn thy mowth ther be no mete,
When thou begynnyst to drynke or speke.
When thou syst any mon drynkynge,
That taketh hed to thy carpynge,
Sone anonn thou sese thy tale,
Whether he drynke wyn other ale.
Loke also thou scorne no mon,
Yn what degrß thou syst hym gon;
Ny thou schalt no mon deprave,
[G]ef thou wolt thy worschepe save;
For suche worde myght ther outberste,

LXIII.
That might make thee sit in evil rest.
Close thy hand in thy fist,
And keep thee well from "had I known."
Hold thy tongue and spend thy sight;
In chamber, among the ladies bright,
Laugh thou not with no great cry,
Nor make no lewd sport and ribaldry.
Play thou not but with thy peers,
Nor tell thou not all that thou hears;
Discover thou not thine own deed,
For no mirth, nor for no reward;
With fair speech thou might have thy will,
With it thou might thy self spoil.

LXIII.
That myg[h]t make the sytte yn evel reste,
Close thy honde yn thy fyste,
And kepe the wel from "had-y-wyste."
Yn chamber amonge the ladyes bryght,
Holde thy tonge and spende thy syght;
Lawge thou not with no gret cry,
Ny make no ragynge with rybody.
Play thou not buyt with thy peres,
Ny tel thou not al that thou heres;
Dyskever thou not thyn owne dede,
For no merthe, ny for no mede;
With fayr speche thou myght have thy wylle,
With hyt thou myght thy selven spylle.

When thou meetest a worthy man,
Cap and hood thou hold not on;
In church, in market, or in the gate,
Do him reverance after his state.
If thou goest with a worthier man
Then thyself thou art one,
Let thy foremost shoulder follow his back,
For that is nurture without lack;
When he doth speak, hold thee still,
When he hath done, say for thy will,
In thy speech that thou be discreet,
And what thou sayest consider thee well;
But deprive thou not him his tale,
Neither at the wine nor at the ale.
Christ then of his high grace,
Save you both wit and space,
Well this book to know and read,
Heaven to have for your reward.
Amen! Amen! so mote it be!
So say we all for charity.

When thou metyst a worthy mon,
Cappe and hod thou holle not on;
Yn churche, yn chepyns, or yn the gate,
Do hym revera(n)s after hys state.
[G]ef thou gost with a worthyor mon
Then thyselven thou art won,
Let thy forther schulder sewe hys backe,
For that ys norter withoute lacke;
When he doth speke, holte the stylle,
When he hath don, sey for thy wylle;
Yn thy speche that thou be felle,
And what thou sayst avyse the welle;
But byref thou not hym hys tale,
Nowther at the wyn, ny at the ale.
Cryst then of hys hye grace,
[G]eve gow bothe wytte and space,
Wel thys boke to conne and rede,
Heven to have for gowre mede.
Amen! amen! so mot hyt be!
Say we so all per charyté

www.ingramcontent.com/pod-product-compliance
Lightning Source LLC
Chambersburg PA
CBHW060855050426
42453CB00008B/980